FROM SEA to SHINING SEA

NORTH DAKOTA

ROBIN L. SILVERMAN

Consultants

MELISSA N. MATUSEVICH, PH.D.

Curriculum and Instruction Specialist
Blacksburg, Virginia

MARY REINERTSON-SAND, M.L.S.

UND College of Nursing, Learning Resource Center
Grand Forks, North Dakota

CHILDREN'S PRESS®

AN IMPRINT OF SCHOLASTIC INC.

New York · Toronto · London · Auckland · Sydney · Mexico City
New Delhi · Hong Kong · Danbury, Connecticut

North Dakota is a Midwestern state. It is bordered by Minnesota; South Dakota; Montana; and the Canadian provinces of Manitoba and Saskatchewan.

The photograph on the front cover shows wildflowers blooming in the wild terrain of North Dakota's Badlands along East River Road, south of Medora.

Project Editor: Meredith DeSousa
Art Director: Marie O'Neill
Photo Researcher: Marybeth Kavanagh
Design: Robin West, Ox and Company, Inc.
Page 6 map and recipe art: Susan Hunt Yule
All other maps: XNR Productions, Inc.
Recipe p. 57 by AlVerne Bohn. Reprinted with permission from *Bread of Life*, p. 319.

Library of Congress Cataloging-in-Publication Data

Silverman, Robin Landew.
   North Dakota / by Robin L. Silverman.
     p. cm. — (From sea to shining sea)
Summary: Describes the geography, history, government, people, and tourist sights of North Dakota.
Includes bibliographical references and index.
   ISBN-10 0-531-21140-1
   ISBN-13 978-0-531-21140-3
   1. North Dakota—Juvenile literature. I. Title. II. Series.
   F636.3 .S55 2009
   978.4—dc22   2008020534

TABLE of CONTENTS

CHAPTER

ONE   Introducing the Peace Garden State.........................4

TWO   The Land of North Dakota...........................7

THREE   North Dakota Through History...........................22

FOUR   Governing North Dakota...........................44

FIVE   The People and Places of North Dakota.................54

North Dakota Almanac...........................70

Timeline...........................72

Gallery of Famous North Dakotans.....................74

Glossary...........................75

For More Information...........................76

Index...........................77

CHAPTER ONE

INTRODUCING THE PEACE GARDEN STATE

North Dakotan Lynell Sandvick surveys the majestic Badlands landscape of western North Dakota.

North Dakota is a bountiful land known by many names. It officially became known as the Peace Garden State when a flower garden, called the International Peace Garden, was created in Dunseith to symbolize peace between the United States and Canada. North Dakota has also been called the Roughrider State in honor of Theodore Roosevelt, a former United States president who spent many years there. During the Spanish-American War, people called Roosevelt's wild volunteer cavalry of riders and riflemen the Rough Riders. North Dakota has also been called the Flickertail State after the ground squirrel, which has a habit of flicking its tail back and forth.

Although it is called by many names, one thing is certain: North Dakota is full of beauty and excitement. It has called to the hearts of explorers and pioneers in every age. Explorers Lewis and Clark spent more than 140 days in North Dakota as they searched for a water passage to the Pacific Ocean. Fur trappers and big game hunters found a treasure trove of bison, bear, elk, moose, and deer. Early American settlers inched their wagon trains over rocks and high prairie grasses before turning the soil into some of the most fertile farmland on earth.

North Dakota's spirit of adventure has helped shape the careers of people like Phil Jackson, coach of the Chicago Bulls and the Los Angeles Lakers. Western fiction writer Louis L'Amour was a North Dakotan, and so was Era Bell Thompson, former editor of *Ebony* magazine, a major national publication. Also, baseball great Roger Maris grew up in Fargo.

What else comes to mind when you think of North Dakota?

* Amber waves of grain on prairie farms
* Explorers Lewis and Clark, and Sacagawea
* Ice fishing and snowmobiling
* Native American powwows
* Norwegian, Icelandic, and other Scandinavian festivals
* Pilots from around the world training at the John D. Odegard School of Aerospace Sciences
* Cowboys and rodeos
* Wind turbines and modern-day coal mining

North Dakota will surprise you. Come explore its windswept plains, jagged hills and buttes, and the colorful International Peace Garden. Turn the page—your adventure is about to begin!

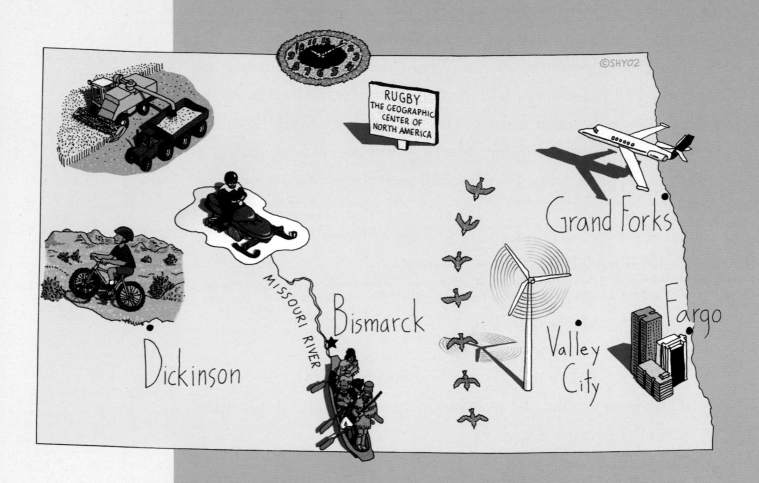

RUGBY
THE GEOGRAPHIC
CENTER OF
NORTH AMERICA

©SHY02

Grand Forks

MISSOURI RIVER

Bismarck

Dickinson

Valley
City

Fargo

CHAPTER TWO

THE LAND OF NORTH DAKOTA

North Dakota is in the north-central part of the United States. Minnesota borders North Dakota to the east. Montana lies to the west and South Dakota to the south. North Dakota's northern neighbor is Canada, and its border touches two Canadian provinces: Manitoba and Saskatchewan.

Within its borders, North Dakota is a land of great diversity. In the east, it is completely flat. The middle of the state has hills and mountains. Much of the west is covered with rocky buttes and canyons. There are three main land regions in North Dakota: the Red River Valley, the Drift Prairie, and the Missouri Plateau or Badlands.

North Dakota is filled with dramatic scenery. Above, a prairie seems to become one with the horizon.

EXTRA! EXTRA!

The geographic center of the continental United States and Canada is just 15 miles (24 kilometers) southwest of Rugby. This spot is equidistant from the Pacific and Atlantic coasts. It is also at the center of the main north-south arc of the continent, which stretches from the northern edge of Canada to the U.S.-Mexican border.

THE RED RIVER VALLEY

The eastern third of North Dakota was shaped by Lake Agassiz, a giant body of water that came from a glacier. What is now known as the Red River Valley was actually a hollow in the earth that held the water, known as the basin of the lake. When the glacier retreated, it left behind soil enriched by the plant and marine life of the water. This black soil is some of the most fertile farmland on earth.

Farm fields in North Dakota are divided into squares called sections. Below, sections of wheat have been planted alongside other crops.

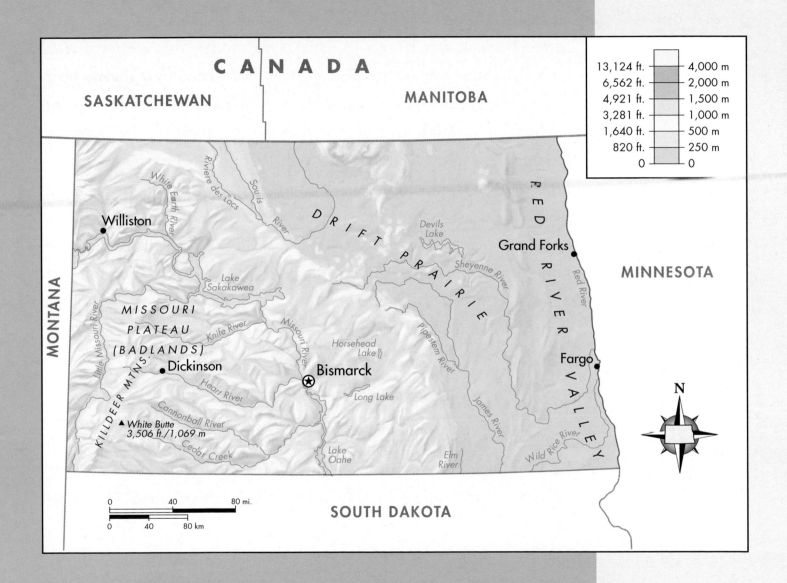

CANADA

SASKATCHEWAN

MANITOBA

MINNESOTA

MONTANA

Williston

White Earth River

Rivière des Lacs

Souris River

DRIFT PRAIRIE

Devils Lake

Grand Forks

Sheyenne River

RED RIVER VALLEY

Red River

Lake Sakakawea

MISSOURI PLATEAU (BADLANDS)

Little Missouri River

Knife River

Missouri River

Horsehead Lake

Pipestem River

Fargo

KILLDEER MTNS.

Dickinson

Heart River

Bismarck

Long Lake

James River

▲ White Butte
3,506 ft./1,069 m

Cannonball River

Cedar Creek

Lake Oahe

Elm River

Wild Rice River

N

0   40   80 mi.

0   40   80 km

SOUTH DAKOTA

13,124 ft.   4,000 m
6,562 ft.   2,000 m
4,921 ft.   1,500 m
3,281 ft.   1,000 m
1,640 ft.   500 m
820 ft.   250 m
0   0

The Red River Valley is extremely flat. When the pioneers first crossed it, the area had very few trees. It looked like a vast sea of grass, some of which was 10 feet (3 meters) tall. Today, this area is covered with fields and rows of specially planted trees known as shelter belts. These trees protect the fields and farms from harsh winds.

Because the land is so flat, flooding can be a problem. Every spring, melting snow in the fields flows into the Red River. The river often overflows its banks and starts moving into the surrounding towns. Even places miles away from the river cannot avoid flooding. Because the water table (water beneath the surface) is very high, melting snow and rainwater cannot always drain completely into the soil. When this happens, it is called overland flooding, and it can be as powerful and destructive as any river flood.

THE DRIFT PRAIRIE

The Drift Prairie lies west of the Red River Valley. A wide variety of landforms can be seen in this region. It has rolling hills and wide-open grasslands, lakes, and ponds. In the north, the prairie turns to forested mountains.

The drift plains have a thick layer of silt that is actually very rich soil. This land is good for farming. It is also a bird lover's paradise. The drift prairie has many potholes and sloughs (pronounced "slews"), which are natural indentations in the land that collect water. As a result, they are perfect places for migratory birds to visit or nest.

THE BADLANDS

The Badlands are part of the Missouri Plateau, an area that covers much of the western parts of North Dakota and South Dakota. The name comes from the Sioux Indians, who called it *mako sica* ("land bad"). French explorers called it *les mauvais terres a traverser* ("bad land to travel across"). This is because the Badlands are filled with canyons, buttes (steep-sided hills), and steep ridges.

Kelly's Slough is a wildlife and wetland preserve that is home to many waterfowl and songbirds.

The Badlands are different from most mountain ranges. When you come upon them, you look down, not up. As you do, you see all kinds of "breaks" in the land. These breaks create bluffs (high, steep hills) and pinnacles (sharp, pointy rock formations). Both bluffs and pinnacles are made of sandstone or limestone that continues to be eroded, or worn away, by wind, rain, hail, and snow.

The Badlands are filled with flint, a very hard rock, and petrified wood. Petrified wood comes from trees like the sycamore and palm, which once grew there. Petrified wood is hard like a rock, because over time, the wood became filled with minerals from the earth and water.

The Badlands are also known for their fossils—hardened remains of plants and animals that once lived there. Scientists have identified more than fourteen dinosaur species that once lived in the state. These include the triceratops and tyrannosaurus rex. Crocodiles and alligators also lived in North Dakota.

This leaf fossil was one of many fossils uncovered in the North Dakota Badlands in June 2002.

WHO'S WHO IN NORTH DAKOTA?

Theodore (Teddy) Roosevelt (1858–1919) helped make the Badlands famous. From 1883 to 1886, he often visited the area before he became president of the United States. He owned two cattle ranches and between 3,000 and 5,000 cattle that grazed freely in the area. Twice a year, he participated in roundups to brand his cattle so they could be distinguished from those owned by other ranchers, whose cattle also roamed the land freely.

The Badlands include the Killdeer Mountains, which are actually two large buttes that cover a total area of about 115 square miles (298 square kilometers). Within these mountains lies a cave called Medicine Hole. According to Native American legend, Medicine Hole is where all the people and animals came out of the earth at the beginning of time.

RIVERS AND LAKES

North Dakota has two large rivers. The Red River of the North forms its eastern border with Minnesota. The Missouri River cuts through the center of the state from Montana on its way south to St. Louis, Missouri.

The Red River is unpredictable. It runs from south to north, beginning in South Dakota and flowing north to Lake Winnipeg in Canada and out to the Hudson Bay. It is very narrow, with many twists and turns. Because the Red River is both shallow and narrow, it floods almost every spring. In 1997, it crested, or swelled to its highest level, at 54 feet (16 m)—26 feet (8 m) higher than its banks. It caused billions of dollars in damage to Grand Forks and other towns and farms in the valley.

The Missouri River is the longest river in the United States. It begins in western

The Missouri River joins with the Yellowstone River in western North Dakota.

Montana and flows south to St. Louis, where it joins the Mississippi River. The Missouri is approximately 2,341 miles (3,767 km) long.

North Dakota's three major lakes are Lake Sakakawea, Lake Oahe (pronounced *o-wa-hee*), and Devils Lake. Lake Sakakawea covers about 480 square miles (1,243 sq km). It is the largest lake in North Dakota and one of the largest in the United States, with more shoreline than the entire coast of California. It is a reservoir, or holding "pond," to help provide hydroelectric power to rural areas. Lake Oahe in the south-central portion of the state is also a man-made reservoir, created by the Oahe Dam near Pierre, South Dakota. Like Lake Sakakawea, Lake Oahe is also very large. It covers about 488 square miles (1,264 sq km).

Lake Sakakawea was formed by the creation of Garrison Dam on the Missouri River.

Devils Lake is North Dakota's largest natural lake. The water level in Devils Lake has been rising since the mid-1990s. Because it has no outlet, it has not only flooded its own shores, but the land of surrounding towns. Almost all the buildings in the town of Church's Ferry had to be moved to escape the flooding. If the waters continue to rise, they could eventually spill into the Sheyenne River, one of the tributaries of the Red River. This would add more water to the Red River each spring, making floods even worse. In 2005, an outlet for Devils Lake was completed over the objections of people who didn't want to abandon lands that would be flooded by the project.

CLIMATE

North Dakota's weather is often extreme. In January, the temperature has dropped as low as –60° Fahrenheit (–51° Celsius), which happened at Parshall on February 15, 1936. Often, it feels even colder than the temperature because of the wind chill factor, a measurement that takes into account the power of the wind. In July, it's just the opposite. Temperatures can reach 90 to 100° F (32 to 38° C). The hottest day on record is 121° F (49° C). This happened on July 6, 1936 in the town of Steele.

Although it gets very cold in North Dakota in winter, the state does not receive

FIND OUT MORE

North Dakota lies at a very high latitude. If you look on a map or globe, you will see horizontal lines that go across a map or in a circle around the globe. These are latitude lines. They measure distance from the equator, or the middle of the earth. Latitude is measured in degrees (°) from 0 to 90. The higher the number, the hotter or colder it can get. North Dakota lies between 45° and 49° north, about halfway to the North Pole. What is the latitude of your state? How does it affect your weather?

North Dakotans enjoy cross-country skiing in the Turtle Mountains.

as much snow as you might think. The annual snowfall ranges from 32 inches (81 centimeters) in the eastern part of the state to just 15 inches (38 cm) in the west. On very cold days, North Dakotans might see colored bands on either side of the sun. These are called sundogs, caused by the sun passing through slowly descending ice crystals.

Most of the state's moisture arrives in spring and summer, usually just enough for farmers to grow their crops. Although the growing season, or time from planting to harvest, is less than 140 days, crops grow

Richardson's ground squirrels recycle soil nutrients and are an important source of prey for many predators. On the other hand, they can destroy crops and spread the bubonic plague.

quickly in North Dakota because summer days have about sixteen hours of sunlight, thanks to the state's high latitude.

ANIMALS, BIRDS, AND FISH

North Dakota has a lively and colorful population of animals, birds, and fish. Bison (also called buffalo) used to roam the land freely, but are now seen only in wildlife refuges, national parks, and private ranches. Moose, wild turkeys, and deer are abundant in the central and western portions of the state. Coyotes prowl the Badlands. Other common animals include badgers, rabbits, foxes, raccoons, skunks, squirrels, and beavers.

The most common animal in North Dakota is Richardson's ground squirrel, named for Sir John Richardson, who first identified it in 1820. It is also known as the gopher or flickertail. Richardson's ground squirrels build deep, complex burrows that can have as many as eight entrances.

North Dakota is one of a few states with a state horse, the Nokota. Today's Nokota horses are descended from feral horses that roamed the Badlands in pioneer days. From 1930 to 1950, government agencies captured and killed many of these

horses because they considered them dangerous. In the 1970s, two brothers, Leo and Frank Kuntz, bought as many Nokota horses as they could to keep them from becoming extinct. Today, the Nokota Horse Conservancy provides land for these horses to roam, as well as feed, water, and shelter during the cold winters.

Bird life is rich and plentiful, especially in the central part of the state. More than 365 different species have been sighted in North Dakota. Large birds like broad-winged hawks and some species of eagles are common. Both snow and Canada geese stop in North Dakota every year on their way south. Mallards and wood ducks are also common

Nokota horses' muscular legs and thicker trunks distinguish them from thoroughbreds and quarterhorses.

sights every fall. Blackbirds, plovers, gulls, hummingbirds, woodpeckers, cuckoos, owls, wood warblers, vultures, and mockingbirds have all been seen in the state. The Western Meadowlark, a brilliant yellow and black bird with a sweet song, is the North Dakota state bird.

North Dakota's lakes and rivers are filled with fish, including pike, perch, catfish, trout, cod, bass, and minnows. Many of these fish have colorful names like the bigmouth buffalo of the sucker family, and the black bullhead of the catfish family. In 1969, the northern pike was named the state fish. It is plentiful in North Dakota waters and can grow to be very large. The largest fish ever caught in North Dakota was a 120-pound (54-kilogram) paddlefish, pulled from the Missouri River in 1993.

FLOWERS AND TREES

(opposite)
Cottonwood trees can grow up to 100 feet (30 m) high, making them one of the largest types of trees in North America.

North Dakota has more than 1,200 varieties of wildflowers, but few types of trees. Most trees can be found in the Turtle Mountains or the Pembina Gorge region in the northeast. The state tree is the American elm. Other trees include the green ash, quaking aspen, birch, and oak. Giant cottonwood trees dot the shores of the Missouri and other rivers. Every spring, cottonwoods release a white, fluffy seed that covers the ground for miles around like a soft blanket.

North Dakota is one of just a few states that adopted a state grass—western wheatgrass. It is found throughout the state, because it can survive both drought (a lack of rain) and floods. North Dakota celebrates its soil, since most of its land is used for farming or ranching. On the North Dakota governor's flag it says, "Strength from the Soil." North Dakotans know that without soil, they cannot grow crops or raise animals for food.

CHAPTER THREE

NORTH DAKOTA THROUGH HISTORY

This buffalo robe, painted by the Hidatsa tribe of North Dakota, is decorated with mounted warriors.

People have lived in North Dakota for more than 15,000 years. These early people, called Paleo-Indians, crossed a land bridge from Siberia to Alaska. They made their way south to North Dakota, where they hunted big game such as giant bison and mammoth and gathered berries and other plant life to eat.

As time passed, newcomers inhabited the area. Some of today's Native American people in North Dakota are descended from three Native American tribes who once lived there: Mandan, Arikara, and Hidatsa. All three tribes lived in different places along the Missouri River, where food and water were plentiful.

The Mandans have lived in the area since about A.D. 1000. They lived in large earth lodges that were big enough for entire families. They raised a variety of crops, including corn, beans, pumpkins, squash, sunflowers, melons, and tobacco. Mandan women were the owners of the earth lodges and tended the crops. The men built lodges, protected their villages, hunted game, and caught fish.

EXPLORERS CLAIM THE LAND

The first Europeans in North Dakota were French explorers. In 1682, René-Robert Cavelier, Sieur de La Salle, traveled down the Mississippi River. He claimed for France all the land drained by the river. This included the southwestern part of present-day North Dakota. France also claimed the northeastern section of North Dakota.

More than fifty years later, in 1738, French fur trader Pierre Gaultier de Varennes, Sieur de La Vérendrye, also came to North Dakota. He was looking for the Northwest Passage, a water route that would make it faster and easier to reach East Asia from Europe. La Vérendrye never found the passage, but he visited many Mandan villages and reported on Mandan society and culture to his king.

LEWIS AND CLARK AND THE CORPS OF DISCOVERY

Most of present-day North Dakota became part of the United States as a result of the Louisiana Purchase. The Louisiana Purchase was a $15 million deal that gave the United States a huge tract of land in the west-

René-Robert Cavelier claimed all of the land drained by the Mississippi River for France. He called the territory *Louisiana*, after the French King Louis XIV.

central part of the country. With this purchase, which took place in 1803, northwestern North Dakota became part of the United States. Fifteen years later, in 1818, the boundary with Canada was fixed and the northeastern section of North Dakota also became part of the United States.

Soon after the Louisiana Purchase, President Thomas Jefferson sent Meriwether Lewis and William Clark to explore the new territory along the Missouri River. Lewis was a United States Army captain and the president's private secretary. Clark had resigned from the army in 1796, but reenlisted in 1803 to join the expedition.

Lewis and Clark and the Corps of Discovery traveled the Missouri River by pirogue, a type of canoe made from a hollowed-out tree trunk. They carried most of their supplies by keelboat, a shallow-bottomed boat that can be pushed along by poles, or pulled by ropes held by men standing on shore. Both the keelboat and the pirogue weighed several tons.

This drawing by Charles M. Russell shows Lewis and Clark meeting the Mandan people in present-day North Dakota.

Lewis and Clark stayed in North Dakota during the winter of 1804–1805. They built Fort Mandan near the shores of the Missouri River. The ever-changing path of the river eventually washed away their fort. Today, a replica (a new building that looks like the original) of Fort Mandan stands near its original site.

Lewis and Clark spent the winter in North Dakota, becoming friendly with the Mandan Indians. There they met French trader Toussaint Charbonneau, who joined their expedition. Charbonneau's wife was Sacagawea (sometimes spelled Sakakawea), a Shoshone woman who became very valuable to the explorers. When the Corps of Discovery ran short of supplies, Sacagawea helped them get food, horses, and guides. She also helped protect the explorers from attacks by Indian tribes because, as Captain Clark wrote in his journal, it was thought that "a woman with a party of men is a token of peace." Sacagawea also showed the members of the Corps how to identify plants and berries that were safe to eat.

A statue of Sacagawea stands on the state capitol grounds in Bismarck.

TRAPPERS AND TRADERS

With its abundant wildlife, North Dakota was a perfect place for hunters. They trapped and traded the hides (skins) of buffalo, fox, beaver, and other animals. Traders took their hides to trading posts, where they traded them in exchange for items such as buttons, thread, pots and pans, soap, and more. The hides were then made into hats, coats, and rugs that were in great demand in American and European cities.

In 1828, Fort Union was built near the Missouri River by John Jacob Astor's American Fur Company. In 1832, the first steamboat arrived at Fort Union, which helped increase both travel and trade up and down the Missouri River. While steamboats moved goods north and south, Red River carts, a supply caravan that crossed the prairie, moved them east and west.

The Native Americans willingly swapped hides, furs, crops, and crafts with the traders. Relationships were so good that some of the white traders married Chippewa women. Their children became known as the Métis, a French word for "mixed."

Métis traders hauled goods between frontier outposts.

Not everything the traders brought to the Native Americans was helpful. In 1837, a disease called smallpox broke out among the Mandan people living near Fort Clark. Although many whites were immune to the disease, the Mandans were not. More than 2,500 Mandan people caught small-pox and died that summer. By the time it was over, there were less than three hundred Mandans left. They moved to the shores of the Knife River to be near the Hidatsa tribe. Eventually, the remaining members of the Arikara joined them, and they became known as the Three Affiliated Tribes.

SETTLERS ARRIVE

The first settlements in North Dakota were established at Pembina in 1812 by Scottish and Irish families, who came looking for free farmland. By 1818, the settlers had built farms, a stockade, the first church, and a school. After Great Britain and the United States established the border between the United States and Canada, a survey showed that the settlers no longer lived in British territory. In spite of all the work they had done, the settlers moved their colony across the border to Canada.

In the early 1850s, the Dakota Land Company in Minnesota and the Western Town Company in Iowa started to buy land in North Dakota for settlements. On March 2, 1861, the United States Congress created the Dakota Territory, which included all of present-day North Dakota and South Dakota and much of Wyoming and Montana. At that time, approximately 2,400 people lived in the region.

To make room for new settlers, the United States government forced Native American tribes to live on reservations. Reservations were areas of land set aside by the government for the use of Native Americans. However, the reservations were

WHAT'S IN A NAME?

The names of many places in North Dakota have interesting origins.

Name	Comes From or Means
Medora	Wife of Antoine de Vallombrosa, Marquis de Mores, a businessman who owned a beef packing plant, stagecoach line, freighting company, and more
Minot	Named for entrepreneur Henry D. Minot
Sacagawea	Means "bird woman," though there is a less accepted theory that her name should be spelled "Sacajawea," meaning "boat pusher"
Dakota	Sioux for "friends" or "allies"
Devils Lake	Miniwaukan term for "spirit water"; early European explorers mistranslated the term as "bad spirit"

This illustration by Frederic Remington shows the Sioux heading into battle.

overcrowded and had poor hunting grounds. The people grew hungry and they resented being forced off their land.

In July 1862, a band of Sioux waged a bloody battle against United States soldiers and settlers in Minnesota, killing more than 400 people and capturing another 300. In response, General Henry H. Sibley and General Alfred H. Sully began a series of devastating battles against the Sioux. Eventually the Sioux were too weak to fight.

To end the war, the United States government signed peace treaties, or formal agreements, with the Native Americans. They promised the Native Americans vast reservations where they could live in peace "as long as the grass grows." Fort Totten became home to the Dakota and Cut Head band of Yankton. Fort Berthold was given to the Three Affiliated Tribes. The Lakota went to the Standing Rock reservation, and the Chippewa and Métis to the Turtle Mountain reservation.

WHO'S WHO IN NORTH DAKOTA?

General George Armstrong Custer (1839–1876) is best known for leading the Seventh Cavalry in the Battle of the Little Bighorn, where Sioux warriors killed every man under his command. Although Custer was stationed in North Dakota, the attacks he led on the Sioux were carried out in Montana and South Dakota.

Despite their promises, the United States government did not respect the treaties. In 1887, a bill called the Allotment Act allowed settlers to take any reservation lands not used by the Native Americans. Some Native Americans sold their land to the settlers, but many more were tricked out of their land.

Even with the Native Americans living on reservations, the government and the settlers still feared them. They considered them savages. Fearing another revolt, the government forced Native Americans to give up their traditional lifestyle and adopt "white" ways in farming, education, and religion. More than one hundred Indian boarding schools were created. Students were forced to attend, even though it meant many had to travel far from home.

RAILROADS AND PROSPERITY

In the mid-1800s, North Dakota became known as a land of opportunity. The "Iron Trail," a nickname for the railroad, opened up as new tracks and trains came through the Dakota Territory.

In 1862, the United States Congress passed the Homestead Act. This act allowed any adult over age 21 to claim 160 acres (65 ha) of land in the Dakota Territory for free. It was required that each person build a house on the land, dig a well, plow at least 10 acres (4 ha), and live there for at least five years.

Advertisements went out all over the country. Settlers came by the tens of thousands to work on the railroad and to farm. Railroad companies

WHO'S WHO IN NORTH DAKOTA?

Sitting Bull (1831–1890) was a leader of the Lakota Sioux community. His Indian name was pronounced *Hun-kesh-nee*, which means "slow," because he was careful about everything he did. He was thought to have great spiritual powers, because he was hardly injured in fierce battles. During a special ceremony called the Sun Dance, he had a vision of soldiers falling from the sky. Not long after, his people defeated General George Armstrong Custer and his men at the Battle of the Little Bighorn. Sitting Bull is considered one of the Lakota's greatest leaders.

Settlers came to North Dakota from many places to help build railroad tracks across the state.

also encouraged people to come to North Dakota. The railroad sold or gave away land along their routes. They wanted as many farms as possible in the region, because riders and freight would create more business for the railroad. By 1890, the population of North Dakota soared to more than 190,000!

One famous railroad man was Minneapolis businessman James J. Hill. He dreamed of building a railroad that would stretch all the way from St. Paul, Minnesota, to the Pacific Ocean. In 1880, one of his Great Northern Railroad trains crossed the border into North Dakota. By 1886, his line reached Minot. By 1893, the Great Northern line reached all the way to the Pacific Ocean. Hill was so successful at bringing both people and prosperity to North Dakota that he became known as the "Empire Builder."

The railroads did not grow without problems, however. In 1873, the Northern Pacific Railway went bankrupt. This meant that they owed people more money than they could repay. To avoid losing money, investors traded their worthless stock for farmland that the railroad owned in the Red River Valley. They hired people to run these enormous farms, which ranged in size from 3,000 to 65,000 acres (1,214 to 26,305 ha). Because of their size and the abundant yields of their wheat crops, these farms became known as bonanza farms. Eventually, the investors earned enough money to continue building the railroad west of the Missouri River. On November 10, 1880, a silver spike was driven into the rail at Sentinel Butte, North Dakota, which was thought to be the border between North Dakota and Montana at that time.

James J. Hill created the Great Northern Railway Company, whose railroad lines became known as the Hill Lines by most people in the West.

Bonanza farms were so large they had to be cultivated by many farmers at once.

FIND OUT MORE

Steamboats and trains were not the only way to get around North Dakota, especially in winter when rivers and lakes were frozen and tracks were covered with snow. Can you imagine a sailboat on skis or a sled powered by a motor and a huge fan? North Dakotans invented these and many other clever ways to get around during winter. How else did they move about?

While the Missouri River brought trade north and south, the railroads helped move people and trade from east to west. Eventually, train travel replaced riverboats as the main type of transportation in North Dakota.

RANCHING DEVELOPS THE WEST

The railroad brought another development to western North Dakota: the sport hunter. Men would ride west on the train, aim their guns out the windows, and shoot buffalo from the comfort and safety of the train cars. Many of these hunters only wanted buffalo heads as trophies for their walls. Often they took only the head and left the rest to waste.

Men hunted buffalo from the windows, platforms, and roofs of railroad cars.

Other nonnative hunters came into the area to hunt buffalo for meat and hides. The meat could be dried, which made it a major source of food during long North Dakota winters. The hides made coats, rugs, and blankets that were perfect for keeping out the bitter cold.

The destruction of the buffalo herds of North Dakota came quickly. In 1882, some 200,000 buffalo hides were carried off to markets in the east. By 1885, the buffalo was almost extinct.

In 1905, President Theodore Roosevelt worked with Ernest Harold Baynes and William Hornaday from the U.S. National Museum to create the American Buffalo Society. By using gifts of land, animals, and money, the Society managed to keep the buffalo from extinction. Today, small herds of buffalo live and breed on private land.

Once the buffalo herds were almost gone, ranchers from as far away as Texas brought cattle into western North Dakota to graze. In the southern part of the United States, cattle were selling for as little as $1 per head, because there were more cattle than buyers. But in North Dakota, a single head of cattle could bring as much as $100 at market because demand was high and supply was low. Cattlemen began to drive their herds north. By the 1880s, more than 500,000 head of cattle were grazing freely in the southern plains of North Dakota, the Badlands, and along the Missouri River.

Unfortunately, a summer drought in 1886, followed by a harsh winter, made it impossible for the cattle to find food. Almost three-quarters of the cattle died within months. Ranching continued, but the land was never overstocked again.

By the early 1880s, hundreds of thousands of people were living in the Dakota Territory. Although the railroads made it easy to travel east and west, it was still difficult to travel north and south. People living in the northern part of the territory began to complain that it took as long to travel to Yankton, the capital of the territory, as it did to go all the way to New York City.

In 1883, lawmakers passed a bill to allow the capital to be moved. Nine towns wanted the honor of becoming the capital, including Aberdeen, Huron, Mitchell, Ordway, Pierre, and Redfield in the south, and Bismarck, Odessa, and Steele in the north. Lawmakers voted thirteen times before choosing Bismarck, which had offered free land for government buildings and $200,000 in cash.

The cornerstone of the capitol was laid in 1883, six years before statehood.

Even before the capital was moved, the people in the southern part of the territory decided they wanted a state of their own. Both North Dakota and South Dakota became states on November 2, 1889. No one knows which is the thirty-ninth or fortieth state, because President Benjamin Harrison wanted it kept secret. However, North Dakota is generally considered the thirty-ninth state because it comes before South Dakota alphabetically. Bismarck remained the capital of North Dakota.

By 1915, more than 350,000 immigrants from European countries had settled in North Dakota. They came from many places, although most were from northern Scandinavian countries such as Norway, Sweden, Finland, and Iceland. These people were used to cold climates, so North Dakota's winters felt natural to them.

Even though their farms produced abundant crops, many farmers were not happy. The big railroad companies that controlled the bonanza farms were unfair to small, independent farmers. For example, small farmers were charged four times as much money to haul their grain to market as farmers on the big bonanza farms. In addition, small farmers were often paid less than big farmers for the same kind of grain. These practices helped railroads and big businesses earn more money, but they hurt people who were trying to survive on their own.

To help the independent farmers, the Non-Partisan League (NPL) was formed by Arthur C. Townley in 1915. The NPL helped to establish a state-run mill and grain elevator, places that would allow independent farmers to save on shipping costs and get fair prices for their wheat. The NPL also created a state highway commission—a group of people to design and oversee the construction of roads in the state—and provided more money for education in rural areas.

North Dakota farmer Arthur C. Townley encouraged 40,000 other farmers to join the Non-Partisan League.

THE DEPRESSION AND BEYOND

In 1929, the stock market collapsed. The years following became known as the Great Depression. All around the United States, businesses closed, people lost their jobs, and many lost their homes when they could no longer afford them.

The Great Depression affected North Dakota, too. Grain prices fell. Many farmers had borrowed money from banks during the 1920s and they could no longer pay their loans, which caused many banks to close. Countless farm families left the state in search of work. When they did, the small-town businesses that served their needs closed, too. Entire communities disappeared, never to be rebuilt.

The remaining farmers faced hard times during the "Dirty Thirties." Dust storms blew away the topsoil, sometimes blocking out the sun for more than a day. Drought affected plant growth. Pests such as cut worms and grasshoppers ate away at the remaining crops.

Perhaps the best thing to happen to North Dakotans at this time was the creation of the International Peace Garden. Canada and the United States had lived

A mother and her children sit outside their drought-stricken farm in North Dakota in 1936.

peacefully for many years, sharing the longest unfortified (unprotected) border of any two nations in the world. To celebrate that fact, Dr. Henry Moore of Canada joined with the National Association of Gardeners in the United States to raise money for the creation of a peace garden. Dunseith was chosen as the site because it is halfway between the Atlantic and Pacific oceans, along what Moore called "The Main Street of the Americas," a route that extends from Cape Horn in South America to Canada.

The garden was dedicated in 1932. The Civilian Conservation Corps (CCC), part of President Franklin D. Roosevelt's plan to put Americans back to work, built many of the structures in the garden. Today, the International Peace Garden has more than 150,000 flowers, including a clock made entirely of flowers. It also features a building with quotations about peace from famous people etched in its walls.

The International Peace Garden covers 2,339 acres (947 ha) of flowers and sculptures.

The CCC also built parks and roads around the state. Another group, called the Works Progress Administration (WPA), put men to work constructing playgrounds, golf courses, skating rinks, swimming pools, and tennis courts. Workers also built dams, wells, bridges, and airports. At its peak, the United States government employed more than 37,000 North Dakotans in special work programs.

RECENT HISTORY

On December 7, 1941, the Japanese navy launched a surprise attack on Pearl Harbor, a U.S. naval base in Hawaii. Japanese fighter planes destroyed two U.S. battleships and killed more than 2,000 men. The next day, the United States entered World War II (1939–1945) by declaring war on Japan and its allies, Germany and Italy.

Many North Dakotans were against joining the war because thousands of residents were descended from German immigrants. However, many North Dakotans willingly served their country. More than 58,000 North Dakota men and 1,500 women joined the American armed forces, including many Native Americans. Those who did not fight supported the effort by buying war bonds and donating money to the American Red Cross. Some North Dakotans went overseas to help entertain the troops.

The demand for farm products grew with the army's increasing needs. Farmers took their earnings, paid off their debts, bought land, and put money in savings accounts. However, after the war, prices went

Upon its completion, Garrison Dam would become the fifth-largest earthen dam structure in the United States.

down again. Farms began to consolidate (come together), creating larger farms but fewer farmers. This meant that resources could be shared and harvests per farm would be bigger, resulting in higher profits.

In 1944, the Pick-Sloan plan to control the waters of the Missouri River was approved by Congress. In 1947, construction of the Garrison Dam began. The dam was finished in 1950, providing hydroelectric or water-created power that brought electricity to many rural areas for the first time. Seven years later, Lake Sakakawea, the reservoir for the dam, was completed.

In the 1950s and 1960s, air force bases were built in Minot and Grand Forks. A radar base to help detect the movement of planes and satellites was activated in Finley. Thousands of military personnel came to North Dakota to serve their country, increasing the state's population.

The 1950s were also a time of great industrial progress in North Dakota. In 1951, oil was discovered near Tioga. Lignite coal was already being mined in the state. Coal-fired plants were built near Velva and Mandan, and oil refineries (places to clean, or purify, oil for future use) opened in Williston and Mandan.

THE GREAT FLOOD

The biggest event in the state's recent history was the Great Flood of 1997. After a winter that dropped 110 inches (279 cm) of snow on the prairie, an April ice storm caused power lines to break down, leaving most of the Red River valley without electricity for up to two weeks. In the meantime, the snow continued to melt. Without electricity, pumps that normally kept houses dry weren't working, and basements started filling up with water. The Red River, which floods its banks at 28 feet (8.5 m), rose to 54 feet (16 m) in just a few weeks.

Almost every town and farm within 15 miles (24 km) of the Red River was affected. Grand Forks and its sister city, East Grand Forks, Minnesota, were the hardest hit. For days, residents worked around the clock building sandbag dikes, or barriers, to protect the city.

In the end, the river won. Grand Forks Mayor Patricia Owens gave the order to evacuate all 50,000 residents of Grand Forks, and East Grand Forks Mayor Lynn Stauss told the 8,000 residents of East Grand Forks that they had to leave, too. Even jails and hospitals were emptied. It was the largest evacuation in the United States since the Civil War. Although no one died during the evacuation, the death rate

In April 1997, the Sorlie Bridge was covered by floodwaters, as was the rest of Grand Forks.

41

soared in the months following the flood, particularly among the elderly. Some died of respiratory illnesses related to toxins, mold, and mildew left behind by the floodwaters.

Things were hard for the evacuees. "We've lost everything," resident Bryan Satterwhite said. "We have no money, no home, just ourselves and the clothes we're wearing." The flood destroyed thousands of homes, filling some with water all the way to the rooftops. The water ruined everything it touched because it was toxic, filled with sewage (waste), dead animals, and oil from cars and furnaces. Everything left behind by the floodwaters had to be destroyed or cleaned with an antibacterial bleach solution.

It was weeks before people could return to their homes. Almost every home, business, house of worship, school, and government building suffered some loss. People spent most of the summer cleaning up, piling flood-soaked items out near the street to be hauled away.

Good people from all over the nation helped rebuild Grand Forks. Some came to build houses and fix basements. Others sent money to churches and schools. Many offered prayers and letters of support. One woman became

A fire broke out after the city flooded, destroying eleven buildings in downtown Grand Forks.

known as The Angel because she donated more than $20 million to help people rebuild their homes.

In 2002 Grand Forks commemorated the fifth anniversary of the flood. Downtown Grand Forks boasts a new farmer's market, refurbished stores and apartments, and several new parks with sculpture and art commemorating the flood. Schools have been rebuilt or replaced. New neighborhoods have been built, filled with both old and new residents. The city continues to grow, slowly but surely.

As North Dakota faces its future, water control remains an issue. Although dikes, or walls, are being built around Grand Forks, no one ever wants to see a major flood again. The Energy and Environmental Research Center at the University of North Dakota is trying to implement a "waffle plan" that would hold melting snow and rainwater in farmers' fields for short periods of time so the Red River does not become overfilled again. In addition, new sources of energy, such as wind power, are being developed in hopes that North Dakota will become an energy leader in the coming decades.

CHAPTER FOUR

GOVERNING NORTH DAKOTA

A monument dedicated to pioneer families stands on the capitol grounds.

North Dakota's state constitution, which contains the laws of how the state will be run, was adopted in 1889. Many of these laws still apply today, more than one hundred years later. However, if any of its laws no longer serve the best interests of the people, the constitution may be amended, or changed. This has been done many times in the history of the state.

North Dakota's government has three branches, or parts: executive, legislative, and judicial. Each of these branches is made up of people who are elected by the citizens of North Dakota. If someone does not do a good job, he or she can be voted out of office when his or her term is up. Together, the three branches take care of running the state and resolving disagreements between its citizens. All three branches have equal power. The three-layered system allows laws to be made or updated, criminals to be brought to justice, and civil matters to be resolved peacefully.

EXECUTIVE BRANCH

The executive branch is responsible for enforcing the laws of North Dakota. The governor is head of the executive branch. He or she is elected by the people for a period of four years. The governor's job is to see that the state's business runs smoothly and that the laws of the state are carried out. The governor is also commander-in-chief of the state's military forces, which means that he or she has the power to call military troops into action in case of emergency.

Although the governor is separate from the legislative branch, which creates laws, he or she does have a say in whether a proposed new law (called a bill) will be passed. In order for a bill to become law, the governor must sign it to indicate his or her approval.

Other officials in the executive branch include the lieutenant governor, who takes the governor's place in case he or she leaves office. The attorney general is the state's main lawyer. He or she works with other lawyers to make sure the state's laws are correctly applied to business problems. North Dakota also has commissioners, or people in charge of matters such as agriculture, insurance, tax, and labor. The lieutenant governor, attorney general, and commissioners are elected by the people.

LEGISLATIVE BRANCH

The legislative branch is made up of two houses, or groups: the senate and the house of representatives. North Dakota has forty-nine senators and ninety-eight representatives. They are elected to four-year terms. Members of this branch, called legislators, pass laws that uphold the

When the legislature is in session, the house chamber (above) is filled with representatives discussing new laws.

state's constitution. To do this, they create bills that are put to a vote.

In order to become a law, a bill must receive more than half the votes of both legislative houses. It is then sent to the governor for his or her approval. If the governor does not like a bill, he or she may veto it, or refuse to sign it into law. Legislators may override (reject) the governor's veto if two-thirds of the members of both the senate and the house of representatives vote for it.

JUDICIAL BRANCH

The judicial branch is where North Dakotans resolve problems related to the law. When people have disagreements, they come to court to find solutions. When someone breaks the law, he or she is brought to court to receive punishment. The courts provide justice or fairness for those who have been harmed.

The judicial branch is made up of different types of courts: a supreme court, a court of appeals, seven district courts, and municipal courts. Large towns in North Dakota have municipal courts, which handle cases involving people who break the law within a city's limits.

District courts hear all cases that occur within a group of counties. Criminal cases (when someone breaks the law) and civil cases (when two parties disagree about the meaning of a law) are heard in district court.

If a citizen is not happy with the judgment of the district court, the citizen may appeal to the North Dakota Supreme Court. An appeal is when someone asks for their case to be heard again in a higher, or more important, court. The supreme court is the highest authority in North Dakota. The person who runs the supreme court is called the chief justice. The supreme court has four other justices, or judges. All are elected for ten-year terms.

The Supreme Court building is located near the state capitol in Bismarck.

TRIBAL GOVERNMENTS

Each of the four Native American reservations in North Dakota has its own government. The reservations are considered sovereign nations, which means they have the power to govern themselves. Tribal members are citizens of both their own nations and of the United States. Members of the tribe must follow the laws of the United States, but they are not controlled by state laws. However, they want to work peacefully with all government officials.

Tribes have their own constitutions, which are upheld by tribal councils. The Standing Rock Tribal Council, for example, consists of a chairman, vice-chairman, secretary, and fourteen councilmen who are elected by tribal members. The tribal council chairman and councilmen are elected to four-year terms.

NORTH DAKOTA STATE GOVERNMENT

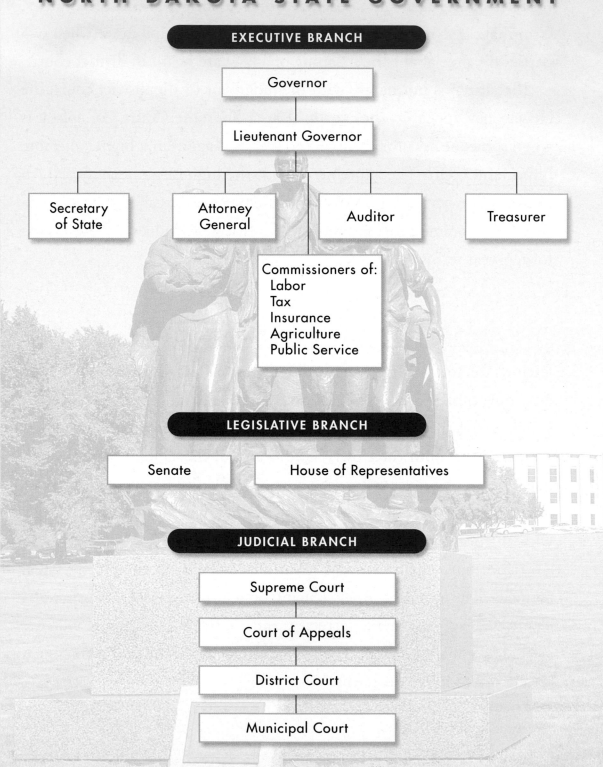

EXECUTIVE BRANCH

Governor

Lieutenant Governor

Secretary of State

Attorney General

Auditor

Treasurer

Commissioners of:
Labor
Tax
Insurance
Agriculture
Public Service

LEGISLATIVE BRANCH

Senate

House of Representatives

JUDICIAL BRANCH

Supreme Court

Court of Appeals

District Court

Municipal Court

NORTH DAKOTA GOVERNORS

Name	Term	Name	Term
John Miller	1889–1890	William Langer	1933–1934
Andrew H. Burke	1891–1892	Ole H. Olson	1934
Eli C. D. Shortridge	1893–1894	Thomas H. Moodie	1935
Roger Allin	1895–1896	Walter Welford	1935–1936
Frank A. Briggs	1897–1898	William Langer	1937–1938
Joseph M. Devine	1898	John Moses	1939–1944
Frederick B. Fancher	1899–1900	Fred G. Aandahl	1945–1950
Frank White	1901–1904	C. Norman Brunsdale	1951–1956
Elmore Y. Sarles	1905–1906	John E. Davis	1957–1960
John Burke	1907–1912	William L. Guy	1961–1972
Louis B. Hanna	1913–1916	Arthur A. Link	1973–1980
Lynn J. Frazier	1917–1921	Allen I. Olson	1981–1984
Ragnvold A. Nestos	1921–1924	George A. Sinner	1985–1992
Arthur G. Sorlie	1925–1928	Edward T. Schafer	1993–2000
Walter J. Maddock	1928	John Hoeven	2000–
George F. Shafer	1929–1932		

Tribal council meetings are held at tribal headquarters, located in the largest town on the reservation. The headquarters of the Standing Rock Nation is in Fort Yates. The Spirit Lake Nation has its headquarters in Fort Totten. The Turtle Mountain Chippewa have their headquarters in Belcourt, and the Three Affiliated Tribes of the Fort Berthold reservation have their headquarters in New Town.

TAKE A TOUR OF BISMARCK, THE CAPITAL CITY

Bismarck is located in the south-central part of the state along the Missouri River. Bismarck was briefly called Edwinton for Edwin Johnson, who helped bring the railroad to the area. In 1873, railroad investors decided to change the city's name to Bismarck in honor of Germany's "Iron Chancellor" Prince Otto Von Bismarck. They hoped that by naming the town after him, more Germans would invest money in the railroad's construction program.

Bismarck is filled with wonderful things to do and places to see. Visitors are welcome to tour the capitol building and grounds, where seventy-five species of trees, shrubs, and flowers bloom every spring. In 1930, the original capi-

EXTRA! EXTRA!

The railroad also influenced the creation of Bismarck's sister city, Mandan. Mandan is on the other side of the Missouri River. It was the logical place to expand the railroad. In 1883, a railway bridge was finished, linking east and west for the first time. The two towns of Bismarck and Mandan have been connected in many ways ever since. Their combined populations make the Bismarck-Mandan metropolitan area the second largest in the state after Fargo.

tol burned down because there was not enough water or long enough hoses to put out the fire.

The cornerstone for a new capitol building was set in 1933, and in 1934, a towering nineteen-story skyscraper replaced the old capitol. Because of its height, some people call it "the skyscraper on the prairie." Other people do not like the rectangular design, since it does not have a dome as most state capitols do. They call it "the silo on the hill," because it looks like the grain elevators where wheat is stored.

The North Dakota Heritage Center is located on the capitol grounds. It houses one of the largest collections of Plains Indian artifacts in the United States. The historic governor's mansion, used until 1960, is also on the grounds and is open for tours.

History lovers will find lots to see and do in the Bismarck/Mandan area. At Fort Abraham Lincoln State Park, visitors can tour the reconstructed home of General and Mrs. Custer and other buildings where the soldiers slept and kept their supplies. Custer Trail Rides are also available for modern-day adventurers who want to explore the bluffs overlooking the mouth of the Heart River.

Camp Hancock is another of Bismarck's military camps, dating back to 1872. It was built to protect Northern Pacific Railroad workers from attacks by the Sioux. Camp Hancock includes a Northern

Costumed actors reenact a cavalry charge at Fort Abraham Lincoln.

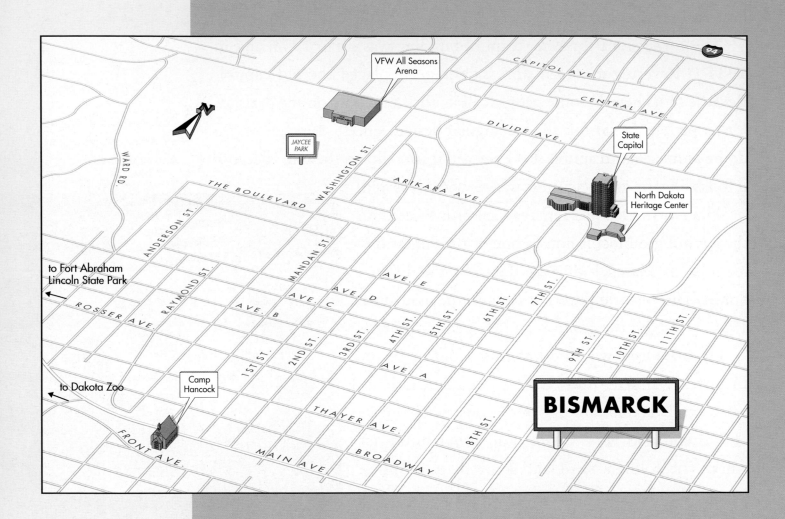

VFW All Seasons Arena

JAYCEE PARK

State Capitol

North Dakota Heritage Center

CAPITOL AVE.

CENTRAL AVE.

DIVIDE AVE.

ARIKARA AVE.

THE BOULEVARD

WASHINGTON ST.

WARD RD.

ANDERSON ST.

RAYMOND ST.

MANDAN ST.

AVE. E

AVE. D

AVE. C

AVE. B

to Fort Abraham
Lincoln State Park

ROSSER AVE.

1ST ST.

2ND ST.

3RD ST.

4TH ST.

5TH ST.

6TH ST.

7TH ST.

9TH ST.

10TH ST.

11TH ST.

AVE. A

to Dakota Zoo

Camp Hancock

THAYER AVE.

8TH ST.

BROADWAY

FRONT AVE.

MAIN AVE.

BISMARCK

94

Pacific steam locomotive and the Bread of Life Episcopal Church as well as an interpretive museum.

Native American history buffs also have plenty to see and do in and around Bismarck. The On-A-Slant Village contains four reconstructed Mandan Indian earth lodges, or homes. The Ward Indian Village Historic Site is a majestic place overlooking the Missouri River Valley. Hundreds of years ago, more than 6,000 people lived in Mandan earth lodge villages there. The site is full of depressions, or hollows, from the lodges and fortification ditches. Seven miles (11 km) north of the city, the Double Ditch Indian Village takes visitors even farther back in history. A self-guided tour describes the remains of a large Mandan earth lodge village that was inhabited between 1675 and 1780.

Bismarck has plenty of other sports and activities, too. The Bismarck Bobcats play fast-paced hockey at the VFW All Seasons Arena. An NBA Development League team, the Dakota Wizards, plays basketball at the Bismark Civic Center. In addition, fairs, exhibitions, and parades keep things lively all year-round in Bismarck.

At one time, about 1,000 Mandan people lived in On-A-Slant Village, a fortified (protected) city.

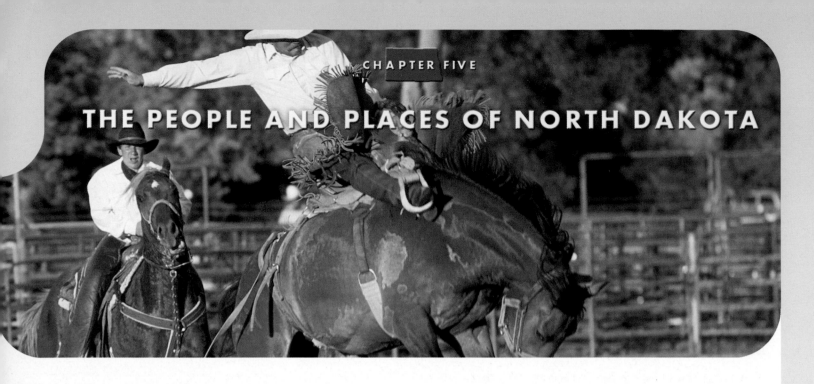

CHAPTER FIVE

THE PEOPLE AND PLACES OF NORTH DAKOTA

Many North Dakotans enjoy participating in the rodeo.

The majority of North Dakotans are descended from farm or ranching families who came to the state in the late 1800s or early 1900s. Some North Dakota families have lived on the same land for as long as seven generations. About 38 percent of the state's population are of Scandinavian descent. About 43 percent of North Dakotans are of German descent. Seven percent of the state's population are of Irish descent.

A small number of North Dakota's residents come from countries such as Bosnia and Vietnam. Many of these people were brought to the state as refugees, people who flee from their homeland because of war or other life-threatening conditions. Between 1996 and 2001, more than 3,000 refugees came to live in North Dakota.

Five in every 100 people in North Dakota are Native American. These include people from the Sioux, Chippewa (or Ojibwa), Cheyenne, Assinboine, Crow, and Cree tribes.

North Dakota has the third fewest people of any state, but it is in the top twenty states for the amount of land within its borders. North Dakota has a low population density, which means it has a lot of land and few people living on it. There are only about nine people per square mile in the state. By contrast, the rest of the United States averages more than 79 people per square mile. Because there is little or no crowding in North Dakota, the stress level is lower and people tend to get along better and live longer. In 1997, an FBI report on crime statistics ranked North Dakota as the safest state in the nation. It also enjoys one of the highest rates for longevity, or how long people live.

Because there is such a great distance between cities and towns, North Dakota has about 434 airports. Many of these are simply landing strips on private land rather than commercial terminals with jets and major airlines. Many farmers and ranchers have their own small planes for transportation, crop dusting, and more.

WHO'S WHO IN NORTH DAKOTA?

Carl Ben Eielson (1897–1929) was a famous aviator. With a fellow pilot, he was the first to fly nonstop over the North Pole. He is known as the "Father of Aviation" in Alaska, where he was first to deliver mail, supplies, and people from place to place using an airplane. Eielson was born in Hatton.

WORKING IN NORTH DAKOTA

North Dakota has three major industries: agriculture, which includes ranching, farming, and related goods and services; mining; and tourism. Almost all of North Dakota's land is either farmed or ranched. In 2000, more than half the land in the state was used for crops, but only 1 in 10 people were farmers. Another one-fourth of the land is used for cattle grazing.

North Dakota ranks first in the nation in the production of eleven crops. These include flaxseed; canola; durum wheat; navy, pinto, and all dry edible beans; spring wheat; dry edible peas; sunflowers; barley; and oats. In late July, the fields are transformed into the "amber waves of grain" that we sing about in the song, "America the Beautiful." Another abundant crop is sugar beets that are processed into sugar. North Dakota is also a large producer of potatoes and soybeans.

Canola is grown in some parts of North Dakota. Canola plants have yellow flowers that produce pods. The seeds of each pod are crushed to make canola oil.

North Dakota's land is rich in fossil and mineral fuels. North Dakota is second in the nation in the mining of lignite, a type of burnable coal that can be turned into gas to heat homes. The nation's largest plant to turn coal into gas is located near Beulah. Although North Dakota only produces one-fiftieth of the nation's oil, it ranks ninth in the amount of crude oil it refines, or processes. North Dakota also has rich natural gas reserves that were discovered at the end of the nineteenth century. Today, natural gas is delivered to other states through huge pipelines.

FIND OUT MORE

North Dakota crops are part of many of the foods you eat. For example, durum wheat is used to make pasta; pinto beans are in chili; and barley may be in your favorite canned soup. What other foods have North Dakota crops in them?

Red-skinned potatoes are grown by many farmers in the Red River Valley. Many of the potatoes grown in North Dakota are turned into potato chips that you buy in the grocery store and French fries that you order at fast-food restaurants. Chances are good that you've already eaten North Dakota potatoes! Remember to ask an adult for help with the recipe below.

BEST-EVER POTATO SALAD

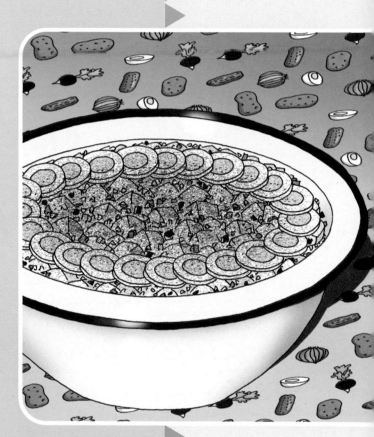

8 cups cooked potatoes, diced
6 hard-boiled eggs (chop four eggs, save two for the garnish)
1/3 cup onion, diced
2 baby dill pickles, chopped
5 radishes, chopped
paprika

Dressing:
1 cup mayonnaise
2 teaspoons mild salad mustard
1/4 cup evaporated milk
1/4 cup sugar
2 teaspoons salt
1/2 teaspoon pepper

Here's what to do:

1. Mix together all salad ingredients except dressing.
2. In a separate bowl, combine all dressing ingredients.
3. Pour dressing over potato mixture and combine. Chill well. Before serving, garnish (decorate) with slices of two remaining hard-boiled eggs. Sprinkle paprika over salad.

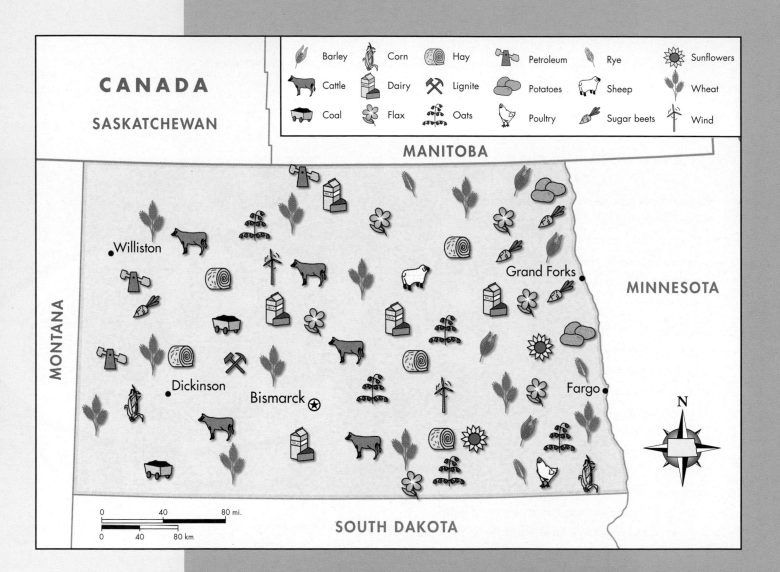

CANADA

SASKATCHEWAN

MANITOBA

MONTANA

MINNESOTA

SOUTH DAKOTA

Williston

Grand Forks

Dickinson

Bismarck ☆

Fargo

Barley
Cattle
Coal
Corn
Dairy
Flax
Hay
Lignite
Oats
Petroleum
Potatoes
Poultry
Rye
Sheep
Sugar beets
Sunflowers
Wheat
Wind

0   40   80 mi.

0   40   80 km

N

North Dakota has another abundant natural resource: the wind. Because the prairie is flat and open, it is common to have windy days in North Dakota. Power companies are now trying to harvest, or use, the wind power with enormous turbines that collect the energy of the blowing wind.

This wind turbine near Valley City can produce enough energy to power 200 to 300 homes.

Tourism is also an important industry in North Dakota. People come from many states and around the world to enjoy the many outdoor activities offered by North Dakota's landscape. Bird-watchers flock to North Dakota every year to see the colorful and spectacular migration that passes over the state. In the fall, flocks of up to one million snow geese at a time fly over North Dakota to their winter nesting places in Texas and Louisiana. Bird hunters come to North Dakota to hunt a small share of the mallards and other common ducks that frequent the prairie sloughs.

Other types of hunting also bring tourists to North Dakota. Fossil hunters of all ages come for archeological digs. Those in search of beauty and good music enjoy the sights and sounds of both the International Peace Garden and the Native American powwows that are held during

Native Americans participate in the Little Shell Powwow at Fort Berthold Indian Reservation in New Town.

EXTRA! EXTRA!

A new type of tourism activity is known as agri-tourism. Some farmers have plowed their wheat fields into mazes that attract both curious people and those who like a clever challenge. Other farmers and ranchers invite people onto their land to ride horses or to help take care of animals or crops. They do these things to bring in more money when crop prices are low.

the warm seasons. Adventurers can hunt down historic sites on the Lewis and Clark trail.

North Dakota's other major industries include services and retail. North Dakotans can be very entrepreneurial, which means that they like to create products and services or start their own businesses. Favorite family recipes have become big sellers over the Internet or in grocery stores. Carol Widman's Candy Company is well known for its "chippers," or chocolate-covered potato chips. The Red Pepper restaurant, a favorite among teenagers in Grand Forks, now ships its unique "grinders" or sandwiches all over the country.

The state also has some manufacturing activity. Manufacturers of farm and other equipment are based in North Dakota. Windows, small airplanes, and software are created there, too.

TAKE A TOUR OF NORTH DAKOTA

Eastern North Dakota

The first stop on our tour is Pembina, in the far northeast corner of the state. At the Pembina State Museum, take the elevator to the seven-story glass observation deck, which gives you a beautiful view of the Red River Valley. The museum is filled with more than 100 million years of the region's history.

Drive down highway I-29 and you'll come to Grand Forks, home of the champion University of North Dakota ice hockey team and the Ralph Englestad Arena, a $100 million facility that is the finest college hockey center in the nation. Next, try the hands-on exhibits at the Dakota Science Center, located in downtown Grand Forks. If you love outer space, take a tour of the John D. Odegard School of Aerospace Sciences and enjoy a star show in the atmospherium. The atmospherium is a multimedia theatre with a huge domed screen where you can experience the feeling of being in outer space during a laser show set to music.

WHO'S WHO IN NORTH DAKOTA?

Harold Schafer (1912–2001) was one of North Dakota's finest entrepreneurs. He founded the Gold Seal Company, which sold Mr. Bubble and other household cleaning products. He started by putting floor wax in cans himself and typing labels for the cans. In his first year, the Gold Seal company made just $900; it later grew to have more than $40 million in sales. Schafer kept a little box on his desk labeled "The Secret of Success." Inside was printed the word *work*.

Then head down the highway to Fargo, where you'll find the Red River Zoo. The zoo features more than three hundred animals from seventy-five species native to Northern Asia and the Great Plains. While you're there, take a ride on the Diederich family carousel. If you love baseball, go to the Roger Maris Museum in the West Acres Shopping Center. There you'll learn more about the Fargo boy who grew up to break Babe Ruth's home run record in 1961. If you're curious about farming, visit Bonanzaville in West Fargo. It is a historic village with cars, machinery, vehicles, and exhibits from the bonanza farm era.

Southern North Dakota

As you head west on Highway I-94 toward Valley City, you'll see an enormous wind turbine near the highway. It's the first in the state to start harvesting the power of the wind to help produce electricity cheaply and cleanly. The wind turbine can produce enough electricity to provide power to three hundred homes.

When you get to Valley City, take a tour of its hills and beautiful historic bridges before you go on to Jamestown, home of the world's largest

The world's largest buffalo draws many tourists to Jamestown each year.

buffalo, a 60-ton (54-metric ton) concrete sculpture dedicated to the American bison. Jamestown is also home to the National Buffalo Museum and White Cloud, a rare albino or white buffalo.

When you get to Mandan, don't miss the rodeo! Mandan Rodeo Days takes place every summer over the Fourth of July holiday. If you're visiting in the fall, be sure to be in Bismarck around Labor Day, when United Tribes International holds one of the biggest powwows in the nation.

While you're in the area, take a detour north to Washburn, where you'll find the Lewis and Clark Interpretive Center. At the center, you can play a trading game where you can swap imaginary buttons and beads for furs and crops. Try on a buffalo robe—it's a lot heavier than

You can see inside a Mandan earth lodge at Knife River Indian Villages.

today's coats! Walk along a dugout canoe made from a cottonwood tree and decide if you would be able to sit in it for a long journey.

Nearby are the Knife River Indian Villages. Go inside a reconstructed earth lodge and see how more than five thousand Hidatsa and Mandan Indians actually lived hundreds of years ago. This is where Lewis and Clark met Sacagawea and her husband, Toussaint Charbonneau. A visitor center has more information about the dwellings, cache (storage) pits, fortification ditches, and trails of the area.

Slightly west of the Knife River Indian Villages is Beulah, where the Freedom Mine is open for tours. It is one of the ten largest coal mines in the United States. Nearby, the Great Plains Synfuels Plant is the country's only commercial-sized plant for turning coal into natural gas. To learn more about the history of these energy sources, the Mercer County Historical Society Museum includes coal-mining equipment from the early 1900s and other displays about frontier life.

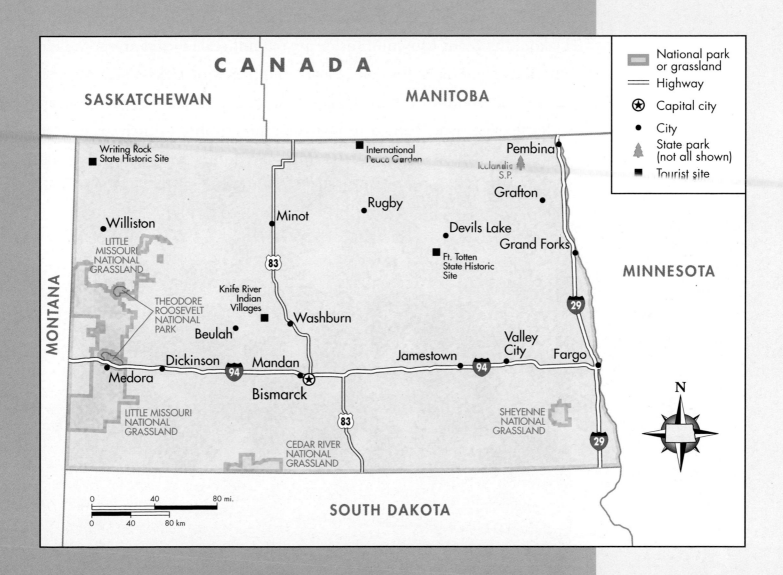

CANADA

SASKATCHEWAN

MANITOBA

National park or grassland

Highway

Capital city

City

State park (not all shown)

Tourist site

Writing Rock State Historic Site

International Peace Garden

Icelandic S.P.

Pembina

Grafton

Rugby

Minot

Williston

Devils Lake

Grand Forks

LITTLE MISSOURI NATIONAL GRASSLAND

MINNESOTA

83

Ft. Totten State Historic Site

THEODORE ROOSEVELT NATIONAL PARK

Knife River Indian Villages

MONTANA

Washburn

Beulah

29

Valley City

Dickinson

Mandan

Jamestown

Fargo

94

94

Medora

Bismarck

LITTLE MISSOURI NATIONAL GRASSLAND

SHEYENNE NATIONAL GRASSLAND

83

29

CEDAR RIVER NATIONAL GRASSLAND

N

0   40   80 mi.

0   40   80 km

SOUTH DAKOTA

Heading west again, you'll come to the town of Dickinson, home of the Dakota Dinosaur Museum. Inside are ten full-scale dinosaurs, complete rhinoceros and bison (buffalo) fossils, and plenty of rocks, minerals, and plants. Just south of Dickinson is the Enchanted Highway, the creation of local artists who wanted to increase tourist traffic to their area. Take Exit 72 and drive along a scenic highway dotted with colorful metal sculptures. Look for the Tin Family, Grasshoppers in the Field, Geese in Flight, and many more.

This triceratops skull is on display at the Dakota Dinosaur Museum.

After Dickinson, welcome to the Badlands! Head into either the north or the south unit of Theodore Roosevelt National Park for horseback riding, hiking, picnicking, camping, or walking among some of the most spectacular scenery you'll see in the Badlands. If you have a bicycle, a horse, or two good feet, see how far you can go on the Maah Daah Hey Trail, a 100-mile (161-km) path that starts south of Medora and wanders through both the north and south units of the park. Be sure to stay up late to watch the spectacular summer sunsets!

Northern North Dakota

Head north from the Badlands and you'll reach Williston, home of the Fort Union Trading Post. You can see how buffalo hides and beaver furs were traded with the Native Americans in exhibits at the reconstructed Bourgeois House. You can even purchase copies of old-fashioned trade goods in the Indian Trade House.

It's worth traveling a few miles north of Williston to see Writing Rock. This is a sacred Native American site that dates back more than two thousand years. The Chippewa call it Hoi-waukon, or Spirit Rock. It is a boulder with images scratched into it. Anthropologists (people who study current and ancient cultures) believe that

According to legend, the future could be predicted by the images on Writing Rock.

the pictures are those of the Thunderbird. The early tribes believed that the Thunderbird could produce both thunder and lightning.

Traveling east, you come to the town of Minot, home of the North Dakota State Fair every July. In Minot, you can also explore a 230-year-old house from Sigdal, Norway, that was taken apart piece by piece and shipped to North Dakota. It sits on the ground of the Scandinavian Heritage Center and Park, which also includes a Danish windmill, a waterfall, and the largest Dala horse in North America. In October, Minot is home to the Norsk Hostfest, North America's largest Scandinavian festival, with activities that honor the traditions of Norway, Sweden, Denmark, Iceland, and Finland.

Rugby is the next city on our tour. The geographic center of North America is marked by a stone cairn, or tower, and a village with historic buildings. The Victorian Dress Museum is also in Rugby. It was created by Marilyn Niewoehner, an expert seamstress. She created thirty-five reproductions of dress styles that were popular in the late nineteenth century. Each dress is sewn from materials that existed more than one hundred years ago. Some of the fabrics cost thousands of dollars, and several dresses took more than a year to sew.

Devils Lake is a few more miles east. Get out your fishing rod—some of the best fishing in the state can be found in its waters. Thirteen miles (21 km) south of Devils Lake you'll find Fort Totten. It is one of the best-preserved military posts in the United States, with seventeen of its original buildings.

Built in 1863, Fort Totten is one of the most well-preserved military forts in the Midwest.

The last stop on our tour is Icelandic State Park. You can boat, fish, or swim on Lake Renwick in the summer, and ski or snowmobile there in the winter. When you're not playing, you can walk inside pioneer buildings to see how families lived in the 1800s. Icelandic State Park also features a 200-acre (81-ha) nature preserve along the Tongue River that is filled with plants, birds, and wildlife. A festival celebrating the Icelandic heritage is held in nearby Mountain every August.

Learn, explore, laugh, and play! You can have it all when you visit North Dakota.

NORTH DAKOTA ALMANAC

Statehood date and number: November 2, 1889/39th

State seal: An oak tree in the center of a field, with a bow and three arrows on the left and a plow and sledge on the right. An Indian on horseback rides toward the sunset. The state motto arcs over forty-two stars. Adopted October 1, 1889.

State flag: A bald eagle holding an olive branch and a bundle of arrows. In its beak is a ribbon with the words, *E Pluribus Unum*, which means "Out of many, one." A shield on the eagle's breast has thirteen stars that represent the original thirteen states. There is a fan above the eagle and a scroll with the state name below it. Adopted January 21, 1911.

Geographic center: Sheridan, 5 miles (8 km) southwest of McClusky

Total area/rank: 70,700 square miles (183,112 sq km)/19th

Borders: Minnesota; Montana; South Dakota; Manitoba and Saskatchewan, Canada

Latitude and longitude: 97° west to 104° west; approximately 45° north to 49° north

Highest/lowest elevation: White Butte, 3,506 feet (1,069 m)/Red River, 750 feet (229 m)

Hottest/coldest temperature: 121° F (49° C) on July 6, 1936 at Steele/−60° F (−51° C) on February 15, 1936 at Parshall

Land area/rank: 68,976 square miles (178,647 sq km)/17th

Inland water area: 1,724 square miles (4,465 sq km)/22nd

Population/rank (2000 census): 642,200/47th

Population of major cities (2000):

Fargo: 90,599

Bismarck: 55,532

Grand Forks: 49,321

Minot: 36,567

Origin of state name: *Dakota* is the Sioux word for "friends"

State capital: Bismarck

Counties: 53

State government: 49 senators, 98 representatives

Major rivers and lakes: Red River of the North, Missouri River, Sheyenne River/Devils Lake, Lake Sakakawea, Lake Oahe

Farm products: Wheat, potatoes, sugar beets, sunflowers, flaxseed, oats, pinto beans, barley, milk

Livestock: Cattle, sheep, hogs

Manufactured products: Farm equipment, food products, excavators and loaders, airplanes, sewer and duct fittings, industrial grade particleboard for construction, windows

Mining products: Petroleum, natural gas, lignite coal, clay, lime, salt, sand, and gravel

Animal: Flickertail (ground squirrel or gopher)

Artifact: Teredo petrified wood

Bird: Western Meadowlark

Dance: Square dance

Equine: Nokota horse

Fish: Northern pike

Flower: Wild prairie rose

Grass: Western wheatgrass

Motto: "Liberty and union, now and forever, one and inseparable"

Nicknames: The Peace Garden State, The Roughrider State, The Flickertail State, The Sioux State

Song: "North Dakota Hymn"

Tree: American elm

Wildlife: Brown grizzly bears, white-tailed deer, antelope, coyote, rabbits, foxes, squirrels, skunks, raccoons, Richardson's ground squirrels, moose, wolves, elk

TIMELINE

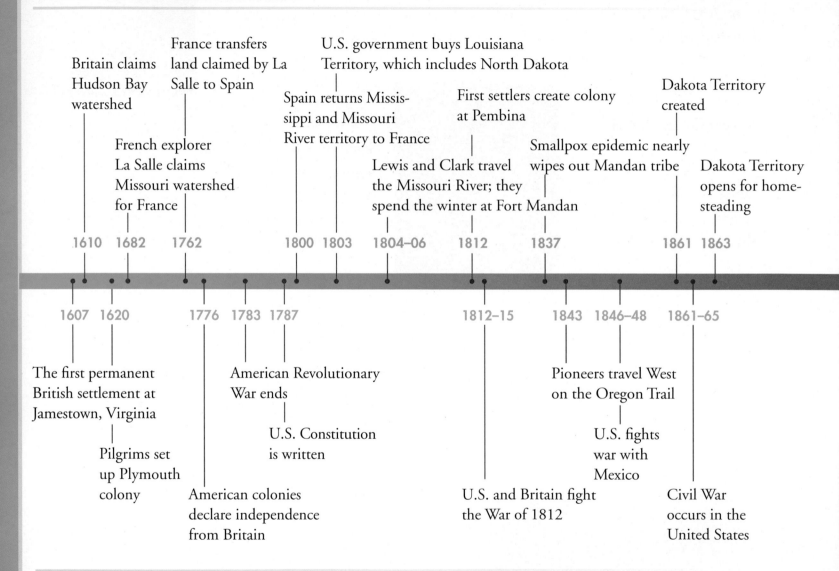

Britain claims
Hudson Bay
watershed

France transfers
land claimed by La
Salle to Spain

U.S. government buys Louisiana
Territory, which includes North Dakota

Spain returns Missis-
sippi and Missouri
River territory to France

French explorer
La Salle claims
Missouri watershed
for France

First settlers create colony
at Pembina

Dakota Territory
created

Smallpox epidemic nearly
wipes out Mandan tribe

Lewis and Clark travel
the Missouri River; they
spend the winter at Fort Mandan

Dakota Territory
opens for home-
steading

1610 1682 1762   1800 1803   1804–06   1812   1837   1861 1863

1607 1620   1776 1783 1787   1812–15   1843 1846–48 1861–65

The first permanent
British settlement at
Jamestown, Virginia

American Revolutionary
War ends

Pioneers travel West
on the Oregon Trail

Pilgrims set
up Plymouth
colony

U.S. Constitution
is written

U.S. fights
war with
Mexico

American colonies
declare independence
from Britain

U.S. and Britain fight
the War of 1812

Civil War
occurs in the
United States

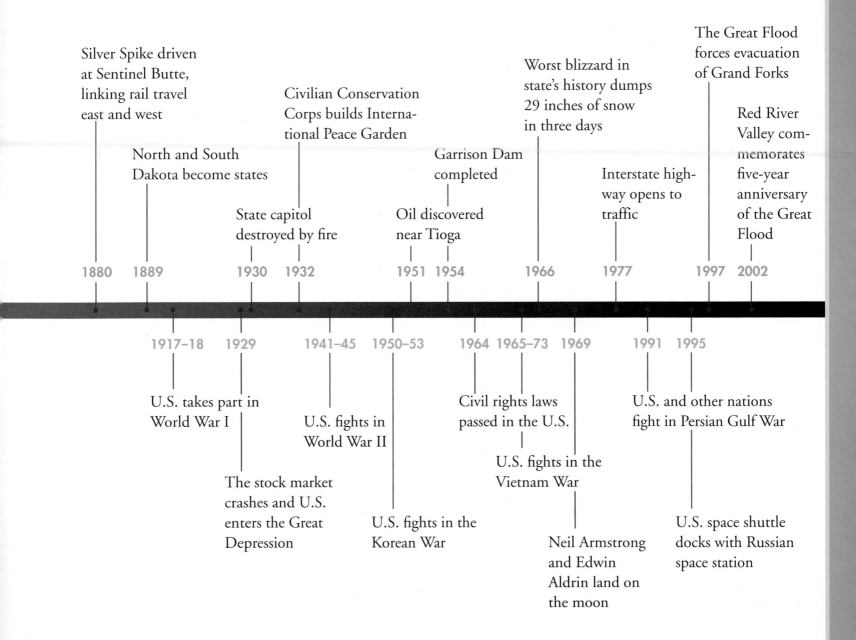

Silver Spike driven at Sentinel Butte, linking rail travel east and west

North and South Dakota become states

Civilian Conservation Corps builds International Peace Garden

State capitol destroyed by fire

Garrison Dam completed

Oil discovered near Tioga

Worst blizzard in state's history dumps 29 inches of snow in three days

Interstate highway opens to traffic

The Great Flood forces evacuation of Grand Forks

Red River Valley commemorates five-year anniversary of the Great Flood

1880   1889   1930   1932   1951   1954   1966   1977   1997   2002

1917–18   1929   1941–45   1950–53   1964   1965–73   1969   1991   1995

U.S. takes part in World War I

U.S. fights in World War II

Civil rights laws passed in the U.S.

U.S. and other nations fight in Persian Gulf War

The stock market crashes and U.S. enters the Great Depression

U.S. fights in the Vietnam War

U.S. fights in the Korean War

Neil Armstrong and Edwin Aldrin land on the moon

U.S. space shuttle docks with Russian space station

GALLERY OF FAMOUS NORTH DAKOTANS

James Buchli
(1945–)
Former NASA astronaut and retired U.S. Marine Corps colonel. Flew on four space flights for the *Discovery* and *Challenger* missions, orbiting the earth a total of 319 times. Born in New Rockford, but considers Fargo his hometown.

Dr. Anne Carlsen
(1915–2002)
Educator born without hands or feet. Became superintendent of Crippled Children's School in Jamestown, which earned a nationwide reputation for excellence.

Warren Christopher
(1925–)
Former Secretary of State for Presidents Carter and Clinton. Helped shape U.S. relations with foreign countries. Born in Scranton.

Angie Dickinson
(1931–)
Actress in more than fifty movies. Best known for television series *Police Woman*. Winner of Golden Globe award. Born in Kulm.

Phil Jackson
(1945–)
Graduated from the University of North Dakota in 1967. Coached the Chicago Bulls and Los Angeles Lakers to multiple NBA Championships. Raised in Williston.

Louis L'Amour
(1908–1988)
Author of 400 short stories and 100 western novels. Born in Jamestown.

Peggy Lee
(1922–2002)
Popular singer and actress. Born in Jamestown.

Roger Maris
(1934–1985)
New York Yankees baseball player who hit sixty-one home runs in 1961, beating Babe Ruth's legendary record by one run. Grew up in Fargo.

Lute Olson
(1935–)
Basketball coach of University of Arizona Wildcats. Born in Mayville.

Cliff (Fido) Purpur
(1912–2001)
Hockey player and coach. First North Dakotan to play in the National Hockey League. Inducted into the U.S. Hockey Hall of Fame. Born in Grand Forks.

Era Bell Thompson
(1905–1986)
University of North Dakota track star who established five women's track records. Author of two books and former editor of *Ebony* magazine.

GLOSSARY

barnstormer: a pilot who does stunts in an airplane

butte: a high hill or ridge, usually with a flat top, that stands alone

cache: a pit for hiding or storing things

earth lodge: large circular dwelling of many Native American tribes before 1900; earth lodges had thick mud walls formed over a frame of tree trunks

endangered: a species that may die out because of conditions hostile to its survival

equidistant: two things that are an equal distance apart

extinct: no longer existing; a species that has died out

feral: once tame (or descended from animals that were tame) and now wild

flickertail: another name for the Richardson's ground squirrel

homesteader: a man or woman who lived on a plot of land given to them by the government as part of the Homestead Act; after living on the land for five years, the land was theirs to keep

pirogue: canoe made from a hollowed-out tree

repeal: to take back or cancel

silo: a tower where grain is stored

slough: a swamp, marsh, or bog where birds often nest or rest as they migrate

tributary: a stream that flows into a larger stream or river

FOR MORE INFORMATION

Web sites

Dakota Science Center

http://www.natureshift.org

A variety of teaching tools about the world in which we live, including history, science, and social studies.

Discover North Dakota

http://www.nd.gov

State government web site.

GreatPlains.org

http://www.greatplains.org

Information about the land and natural resources of the Great Plains.

Discover North Dakota

http://www.ndtourism.com

Information about tourist attractions and places to stay.

Books

Freedman, Russell. *Buffalo Hunt*. New York, NY: Holiday House, 1988.

Thomasma, Kenneth. *The Truth About Sacajawea*. Jackson, WY: Grandview Publishing, 1997.

Webster, Christine. *The Lewis and Clark Expedition*. Danbury, CT: Children's Press, 2003.

Addresses

State Historical Society of North Dakota
North Dakota Heritage Center
612 East Boulevard Avenue
Bismarck, ND 58505-0830

Lewis and Clark Interpretive Center
U.S. Highway 83 and ND 200A
Washburn, ND 58577

Fort Berthold
Mandan, Hidatsa and Arikara Three Affiliated Tribes
CH3 Box 2
New Town, ND 58763

Fort Yates
Standing Rock Sioux Tribe
P. O. Box D
Fort Yates, ND 58538

Turtle Mountain
Turtle Mountain Band of Chippewa
P. O. Box 900
Belcourt, ND 58316

Fort Totten
Spirit Lake Sioux Tribe
P. O. Box 359
Fort Totten, ND 58335

INDEX

Page numbers in *italics* indicate illustrations

agriculture, 17, 21, 22, 31, 35–36, 37, 39–40, 55–56, 70
agri-tourism, 60
Allotment Act, 29
American Buffalo Society, 33
American Fur Company, 26
Astor, John Jacob, 26
atmospherium, 61

Badlands, 7, 11–14, 18, 33, 67
barnstormer, 62, 75
Battle of Little Bighorn, 29
Baynes, Ernest Harold, 33
Beulah, 56, 64
birds, 11, 19–20, 59
Bismarck, 34, 35, 63, 50–53
Bismarck, Otto Von, 50
bison. *See* Buffalo
bonanza farms, 31, *31*, 35
Bonanzaville, 62
Bread of Life Episcopal Church, 53
Buchanan, James, 27
Buchli, James, 74
buffalo, 18, 22, 32, *32*, 33, 63
butte, 11, 14, 75

Camp Hancock, 51
Canada, 4, 7, 14, 24, 27, 37–38
Canola, 56
Carlsen, Anne, 74
Carol Widman's Candy Company, 60
Charbonneau, Toussaint, 25, 64
Christopher, Warren, 74, *74*
Church's Ferry, 16
Civilian Conservation Corps, 38–39
Clark, William, 5, 24, *24*, 64
climate, 16–18, 70
Corps of Discovery, 24–25
cottonwood trees, 20, *21*
Custer, George Armstrong, 27, *27*, 29, 51

Custer Trail Rides, 51
Dakota Land Company, 27
Dakota Territory, 27, 29, 34
Dickinson, 66
Dickinson, Angie, 74
Double Ditch Indian Village, 53
Drift Prairie, 7, 10
drought, 33, 37
Dunseith, 4, 38

earth lodge, 22, 53, *64*, 75
Eielson, Carl Ben, 55, *55*
Enchanted Highway, 66
Energy and Environmental Research Center, 43
equidistant, 7, 75
extinct, 19, 33, 75

famous people, 5, 13, 27, 29, 55, 61, 62, 74
Fargo, 5, 50, 62, 74
festivals and fairs, 5, 69
    Norsk Hostfest, 68
    North Dakota State Fair, 68
flickertail, 4, 18, 75
flooding, 10, 14, 16, 21, 41–43
    Great Flood of 1997, 41–43
Fort Berthold, 28, 50, 60
Fort Clark, 26
Fort Mandan, 25
Fort Totten, 28, 50, 68, *69*
Fort Union, 26
Fort Union Trading Post, 67
Fort Yates, 50
fossil, 13, 59, 66
Freedom Mine, 64

Garrison Dam, 40, *40*
Gold Seal Company, 61
government, 44–50
    executive branch, 45, *48*
    governor, 45, *48*, 49
    judicial branch, 46–47, *48*
    legislative branch, 45–46, *48*

tribal governments, 47, 50
Grand Forks, 14, 40, 41–43, 61, 74
Great Depression, 37
Great Plains Synfuels Plant, 64

Harrison, Benjamin, 35
Hill, James J., 30, *31*
historic villages
    Bonanzaville, 62
    Indian villages, 53, *53*, 64, *64*
history, 22–43
    ranching, 33
    settlements, 27, 29
    traders, 25–26
Homestead Act, 29
Hornaday, William, 33
hunting, 32–33
hydroelectric power, 15, 40

immigrants, 35, 39, 54
Indian Trade House, 67
industry, 70–71
    agriculture, 17, 21, 22, 31, 35–36,
        37, 39–40, 55–56, 70
    manufacturing, 61
    mining, 5, 40, 55, 56
    service, 60–61
    tourism, 55, 59
International Peace Garden, 4, 5, 37–38,
    38, 59

Jackson, Phil, 5, 74
Jamestown, 62–63, 74
Jefferson, Thomas, 24
John D. Odegard School of Aerospace
        Sciences, 5, 61
Johnston, Edwin, 50

Kelly's Slough, *11*
Kennedy Bridge, *41*
Klingensmith, Florence, 62, *62*
Knife River Indian Villages, 64, *64*
Kuntz, Frank, 19
Kuntz, Leo, 19

lakes, 20, 70
    Devils Lake, 15, 16, 29, 68

Lake Agassiz, 8
Lake Oahe, 15
Lake Renwick, 69
Lake Sakakawea, 15, *15*, 40
Lake Winnipeg, 14
L'Amour, Louis, 5, 74
La Salle, René-Robert Cavelier, Sieur de, 23
latitude, 16, 18, 70
La Vérendrye, Pierre Gaultier de
        Varennes de, 23
Lee, Peggy, 74
Lewis, Meriwether, 5, 24, *24*, 25, 64
Lewis and Clark Interpretive Center, 63
Linton, 18
Louis XIV, king of France, 23
Louisiana Purchase, 23

Maah Daah Hey Trail, 67
Mandan, 40, 50, 63
maps
    Bismarck, *52*
    illustrated, 6
    highway, *65*
    locator, *2*
    resources, *58*
    topographic, 9
Maris, Roger, 5, 62, 74, *74*
Medicine Hole, 14
Medora, 67
Metis, 26, *26*, 28
Minnesota, 7, 14, 27, 28, 30, 41
Minot, 30, 40, 68
Minot, Henry D., 28
Missouri, 14
Missouri Plateau, 7, 11
Montana, 7, 14, 27, 31
Moore, Henry, 38
mountains
    Killdeer Mountains, 14
    Turtle Mountains, 17
museums. *See also* Historic villages
    Bourgeois House, 67
    Camp Hancock, 51
    Dakota Dinosaur Museum, 66
    Dakota Science Center, 61
    Mercer County Historical Society
        Museum, 64

National Buffalo Museum, 63
North Dakota Heritage Center, 51
Pembina State Museum, 61
Roger Maris Museum, 62
Victorian Dress Museum, 68

National Association of Gardeners, 38
Native Americans, 11, 14, 20, 22–29,
    39, 47, 51, 53, 54, 59–60, 60,
    64, 67
  Arikara, 26
  Assinboine, 54
  Cheyenne, 54
  Chippewa, 26, 28, 54, 67
  Cree, 54
  Crow, 54
  Hidatsa, 26, 64
  Lakota, 29
  Mandan, 22–23, 24, 25, 26, 53, 64
  Paleo-Indians, 22
  Shosone, 25
  Sioux, 4, 11, 28, 51, 54
New Town, 50, 60
Niewoehner, Marilyn, 68
Nokota horses, 18–19, 19
Nonpartisan League (NPL), 36
Norsk Hostfest, 68
North Dakota State Fair, 68
Northern Pike, 20

Oahe Dam, 15
Odessa, 34
Olson, Lute, 74
On-A-Slant Indian Village, 53, 53
Owens, Patricia, 41

parks
  Fort Abraham Lincoln State Park, 51
  Icelandic State Park, 69
  Theodore Roosevelt National Park, 67
Peace Garden. See International Peace
    Garden
Pembina, 27, 61
Pembina Gorge, 20
people, 54–55. See also Famous people;
    Immigrants; Native Americans
Pick-Sloan plan, 40

pinnacle, 12
pirogue, 24, 75
population, 27, 30, 50, 54, 70
potato salad recipe, 57
powwow, 5, 20, 59–60
Purpur, Cliff (Fido), 74

railroad (railroad companies), 29–32,
    32, 34, 35–36, 50
Ralph Englestad arena, 61
recipe, 57
Red Pepper restaurant, 61
Red River Valley, 7–10, 31, 57, 61
Red River Zoo, 62
Remington, Frederic, 28
reservations, 27, 28, 29, 47
Richardson, Sir John, 18
rivers, 20, 70
  Heart River, 51
  Mississippi River, 15, 23
  Missouri River, 14–15, 20, 22, 24–25,
    31, 32, 33, 40, 50
  Red River, 14, 16, 41, 43
  Sheyenne River, 16
  Tongue River, 69
rodeo, 5, 63
Roosevelt, Franklin D., 38
Roosevelt, Theodore, 4, 13, 13, 33
Rugby, 7, 68
Russell, Charles M., 24
Rutland, 64

Sacagawea, 5, 25, 25, 27, 64
Sandvick, Lynell, 4
Satterwhite, Bryan, 42
Scandinavian immigrants, 35, 54
Scandinavian Heritage Center and Park,
    68
Schafer, Harold, 61, 61
schools, 35
  John D. Odegard School of Aero-
    space Sciences, 5, 61
  University of North Dakota, 43, 61,
    74
sculptures, 25, 63, 63, 66, 66
Sentinel Butte, 31
Sibley, Henry H., 28

silo, 51, 75
Sitting Bull, 29, *29*
slough, 10, *11*, 59, 75
South Dakota, 7, 11, 14, 15, 27, 35. *See also* Dakota Territory
sports, 5, 53, 61, 74
state facts, 4, 20, 21, 28, 70–71
  origins of names, 28, 70
statehood, 34–35
steamboat, 26, 32
Steele, 34
Strauss, Lynn, 41
Sully, Alfred H., 28
sundog, 16

Thompson, Era Bell, 5, 74
Three Affiliated Tribes, 26, 28
Thunderbird, 68
timeline, 72–73
Tioga, 40
Townley, Arthur C., 36, *36*
tributary, 16, 75
turbine, 5, 15, 59, 62

United Tribes International, 63
University of North Dakota, 43, 61, 74

Valley City, 62
Vallombrosa, Antoine de, 28
Velva, 40

Ward Indian Village Historic Site, 53
Washburn, 63
Western Town Company, 27
West Fargo, 62
White Cloud, 63
wildlife, 5, 10, 11, 18–19, 25, 69
Williston, 40, 67, 74
Works Progress Administration, 39
World War II, 39
Writing Rock, 67, *67*, 68

Yankton, 28, 34

ABOUT THE AUTHOR

Robin L. Silverman is the author of *The Ten Gifts*, *Something Wonderful Is About to Happen*, and *A Bosnian Family*. She has lived in North Dakota for twenty-four years with her husband, photographer Steve Silverman, and their two daughters. Robin travels the country as an inspirational speaker, helping men, women, and students everywhere to embrace the adventure of life.

Photographs © 2009: AP Images: 41 (Beth A. Keiser), 55 (Will Kincaid), 13 top (Eloise Ogden), 74 right; Corbis Images: 8 (Annie Griffiths Belt), 3 left, 12 (Sheldan Collins), 74 left (Najlah Feanny-Hicks), 62 (Minnesota Historical Society), 37 (Arthur Rothstein), 42 (St. Paul Pioneer Press/Sygma), 31 top; Craig Bihrle: 51; Dakota Dinosaur Museum/Larry League: 66; Dave G. Houser/HouserStock, Inc.: 63; Dawn Charging: 69; Garry Redmann: 47; Getty Images: 22 (Karl Bodmer/Hulton Archive), 13 bottom, 28 bottom, 32 (Hulton Archive), 14 (Larry Mayer/Liaison); ImageState/Andre Jenny: 53, 60; Institute for Regional Studies, NDSU Libraries, Fargo: 61; MapQuest.com, Inc.: 70 bottom; North Dakota Secretary of State Office: 70 top; North Dakota Tourism Department/Pat Hertz: 25; North Wind Picture Archives: 67 (Nancy Carter), 28 top, 30, 31 bottom, 34; Photo Researchers, NY/Ken M. Highfill: 71 right; Robertstock.com: 71 left (H. Cruickshank), 44, 48 background (R. Gilbert); Sheldon Green: 3 right, 17, 54; State Historical Society of North Dakota: 26, 36, 40; Steve Silverman: cover, 4, 7, 11, 15, 19, 21, 56, 59; Stock Montage, Inc.: 23, 24; Superstock, Inc.: 29 (D.F. Barry), 18; Unicorn Stock Photos: 46 (V.E. Horne), 64 (Andre Jenny); Visuals Unlimited/Tim Hauf: 38.